# Who Carved the Mountain?
## The Story of Mount Rushmore

Mount Rushmore Bookstores

A 2008-2009 Prairie Pasque Award Nominee
South Dakota Library Association

*The author would like to thank Debbie M. Ketel,*
*Bruce Weisman, the Mount Rushmore Bookstores,*
*and the interpretive staff at*
*Mount Rushmore for their warm and generous help.*

*For the faces of the future*
*—JLSP*

*For my family,*
*Tim, Maggie, Max and Misty-dog*
*—RG*

First Printing 2005; Second Printing 2006; Third Printing 2010; Fourth Printing 2016
Published by the MOUNT RUSHMORE Bookstores
Written by Jean L.S. Patrick
Illustrations by Renée Graef
Design: F + P Graphic Design, Inc.
Editors: Mount Rushmore National Memorial's Education Specialist Rhonda Buell Schier and Debbie M. Ketel
Copy Editor: Mary Anne Maier
Project Manager: Debbie M. Ketel
Reviewer: Mount Rushmore National Memorial's Chief of Interpretation Judy Olson
Manufactured by Friesens Corporation with vegetable-based inks
Manufactured in Altona, MB, Canada in 5/2016
Job #220937

Library of Congress Cataloging-in-Publication Data

Patrick, Jean L. S.
    Who carved the mountain? : the story of Mount Rushmore /
by Jean L.S. Patrick ; illustrated by Renée Graef.
        p. cm.
    Includes bibliographical references.
    Audience: Grades K–3.
    ISBN 978-0-9752617-4-3 (hardcover : alk. paper)
    1. Borglum, Gutzon, 1867–1941—Juvenile literature. 2. Stone carvers—
United States—Biography—Juvenile literature. 3. Mount Rushmore National
Memorial (S.D.)—History—Juvenile literature. I. Graef, Renée. II. Title.
    F657.R8P38 2005
    978.3'93'0922–dc22
    2004020505

Mount Rushmore Bookstores · www.mountrushmoresociety.com
13036 Hwy 244 · Keystone, SD 57751 · 1-800-699-3142

As a committee of the Mount Rushmore Society, the mission of the Mount Rushmore Bookstores is to support and assist the
National Park Service with educational, historical, and interpretive activities at Mount Rushmore National Memorial. Your membership in the nonprofit organization
will provide funding for interpretive exhibits, educational programs, and special events at Mount Rushmore National Memorial. Go to www.mountrushmoresociety.com for more information.

# Who Carved the Mountain?
## The Story of Mount Rushmore

BY **Jean L.S. Patrick**     ILLUSTRATED BY **Renée Graef**

PUBLISHED BY THE MOUNT RUSHMORE BOOKSTORES

# These are the Black Hills of South Dakota.

From far away, these hills look black.
But up close, they're dark green.
They are covered with thick forests
    Of spruce and ponderosa pine.

Some of the hills look like mountains.
Huge cliffs of granite burst from the slopes.
Tall rocks called Needles point to the sky.

High in this land, you'll see the faces
    Of four United States presidents.

Why were they carved?
    To represent our country.

How were they carved?
    With dynamite and determination.

This is the story of Mount Rushmore.

    These are the voices of its people....

# MORE OF THE STORY

**Doane Robinson** was the historian for the state of South Dakota. In 1923, he had the idea for carving the Needles.

### Nickname
When Doane Robinson was born, his name was Jonah. But his sister couldn't say it, so she called him Do-nah. The name "Doane" stuck with him for life!

### Location
Mount Rushmore is located in the Black Hills of South Dakota. The Lakota name for the Black Hills is Paha Sapa.

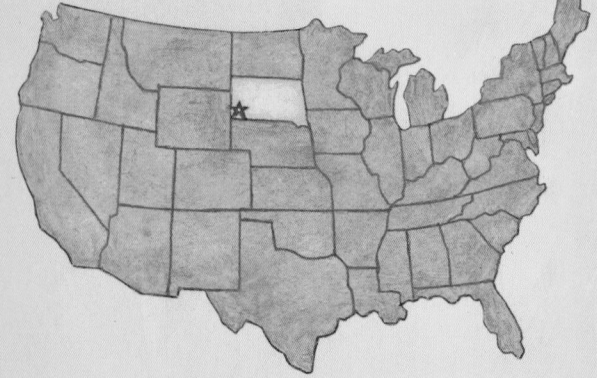

**How did Mount Rushmore get its name?**
In 1885, a lawyer by the name of Charles E. Rushmore was visiting the Black Hills. When he asked his guide the name of the mountain, the guide said, "Never had none. But here-after we'll call 'er Rushmore."

**Who Were the Western Heroes?**
**Buffalo Bill Cody** was a Pony Express rider, a U.S. Army scout, and the leader of his own "Wild West" show.

**Red Cloud** was an Oglala chief who fought for the needs of his people.

**Meriwether Lewis** and **William Clark** explored the West between 1804 and 1806.

**Sacagawea** was a Shoshone woman who served as Lewis & Clark's guide.

**Buffalo Bill Cody**

**Chief Red Cloud**

**Meriwether Lewis**

**William Clark**

**Sacagawea**

# Doane Robinson

My name is Doane Robinson.
I am the man who had the plan
    To carve heroes on a mountain.

I loved the Black Hills of South Dakota.
I wished that people from across the land
    Would come to see their beauty.

I thought of a plan,
    A wonderful plan.
        The Needles could be carved!

I imagined huge statues of western heroes…
    Buffalo Bill, Chief Red Cloud,
        Lewis & Clark, and Sacagawea.

So I wrote to a sculptor and told him my plan
    To carve heroes on a mountain.

        Who was this sculptor?

8

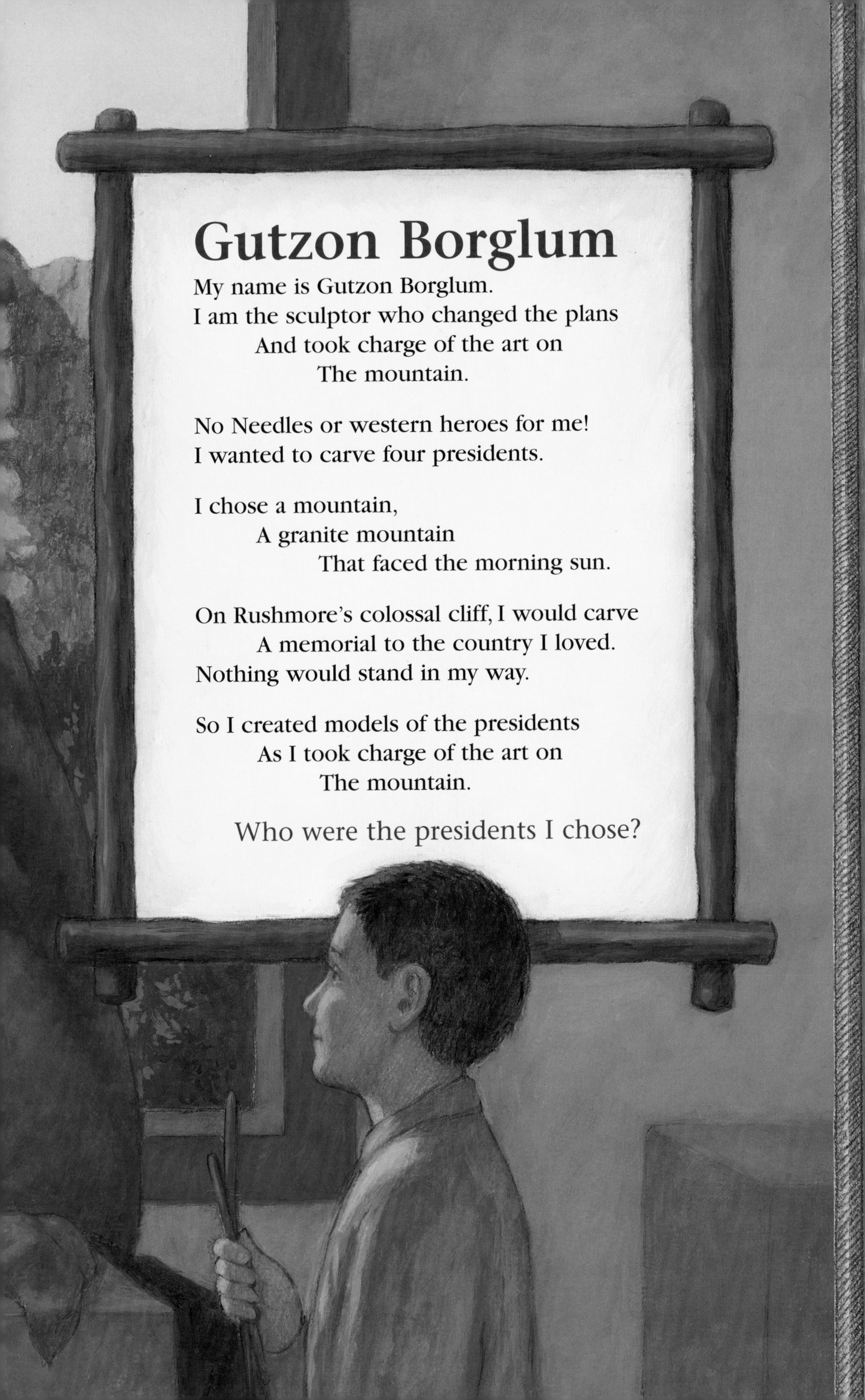

# Gutzon Borglum

My name is Gutzon Borglum.
I am the sculptor who changed the plans
  And took charge of the art on
    The mountain.

No Needles or western heroes for me!
I wanted to carve four presidents.

I chose a mountain,
    A granite mountain
      That faced the morning sun.

On Rushmore's colossal cliff, I would carve
    A memorial to the country I loved.
Nothing would stand in my way.

So I created models of the presidents
    As I took charge of the art on
      The mountain.

Who were the presidents I chose?

## MORE OF THE STORY

**BORN** Bear Lake, Idaho, on March 25, 1867
**FULL NAME** John Gutzon de la Mothe Borglum
**BOYHOOD** Grew up in Fremont, Nebraska
**OCCUPATIONS** Painter, Boxer, Politician, Inventor, Sculptor

**Borglum's Belief**
*"Don't say 'I can't' on this work. The 'I can'ts' are unknown in the world's work and unremembered in history."*
— GUTZON BORGLUM

**Finding Mount Rushmore:** On a horse named "Highpockets," forester Theodore Shoemaker led Gutzon and his son, Lincoln, to Mount Rushmore in 1925. As the story goes, Shoemaker asked Gutzon to keep his eyes shut until they reached an ideal view of the mountain.

## MORE OF THE STORY

BORN February 22, 1732
BIRTHPLACE Westmoreland County, Virginia
HEIGHT "Six feet two inches in his stockings"
DIED December 14, 1799
BURIED Mount Vernon, Virginia

### Career Highlights

Served as Commander-in-Chief of the Continental Army from 1775 to 1783.

Led the thirteen colonies in the fight for independence from Britain.

Presided over the Constitutional Convention in 1787.

Helped create rules and principles of the Constitution.

Served as first president of the United States from 1789 to 1797.

### Democracy

In a *democracy*, people have the power to choose their leaders and to participate in their government. In the United States, people continue to follow the democratic principles of the Constitution.

*"The welfare of our Country is the great object to which our cares and efforts ought to be directed."*

– GEORGE WASHINGTON
January 8, 1790

### Interesting Fact

George Washington had false teeth, but they weren't wooden. They were made from gold, ivory, lead and animal teeth.

**Inauguration:** George Washington took the Presidential Oath of Office in 1789.

10

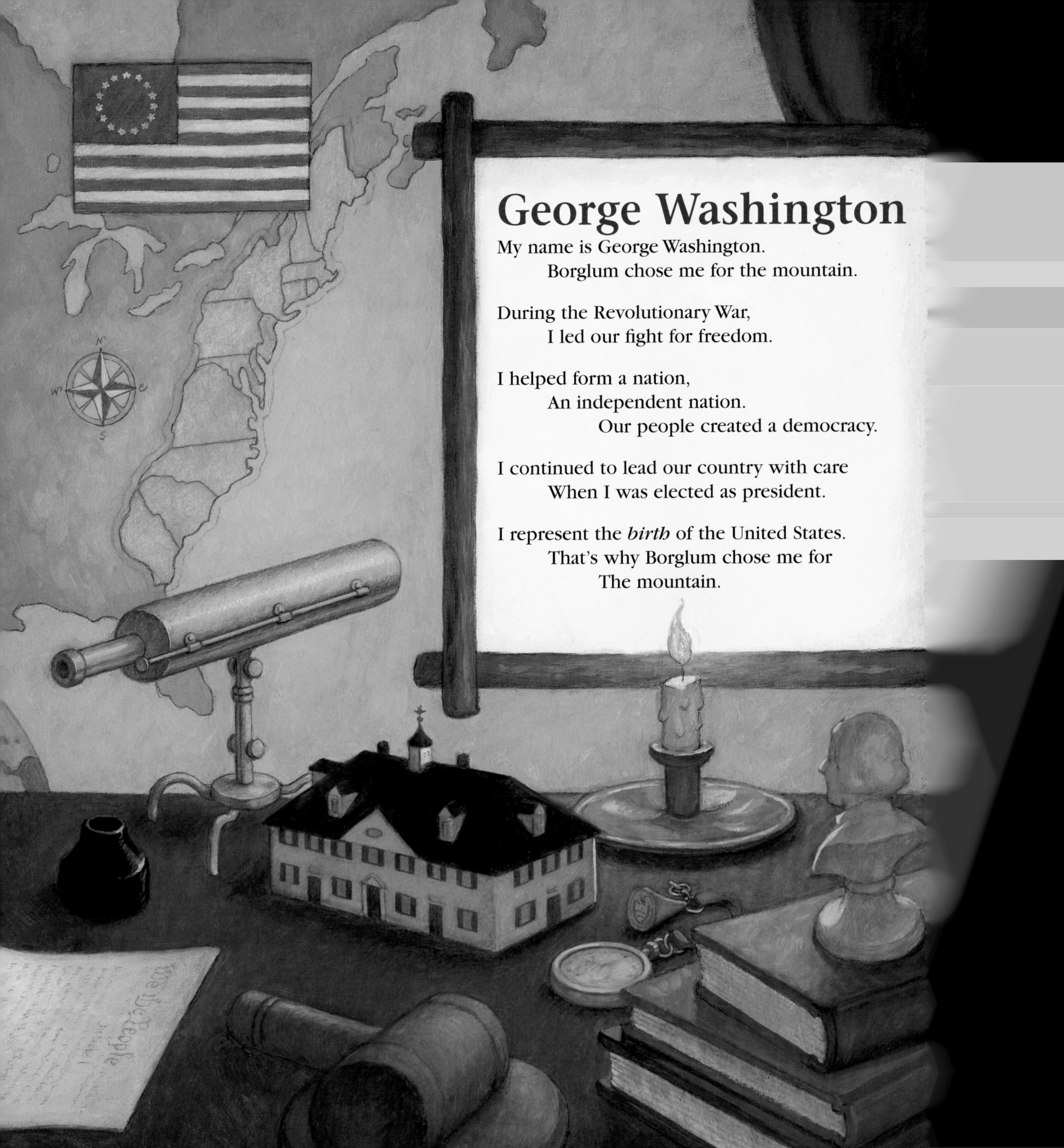

# George Washington

My name is George Washington.
    Borglum chose me for the mountain.

During the Revolutionary War,
    I led our fight for freedom.

I helped form a nation,
    An independent nation.
        Our people created a democracy.

I continued to lead our country with care
    When I was elected as president.

I represent the *birth* of the United States.
    That's why Borglum chose me for
        The mountain.

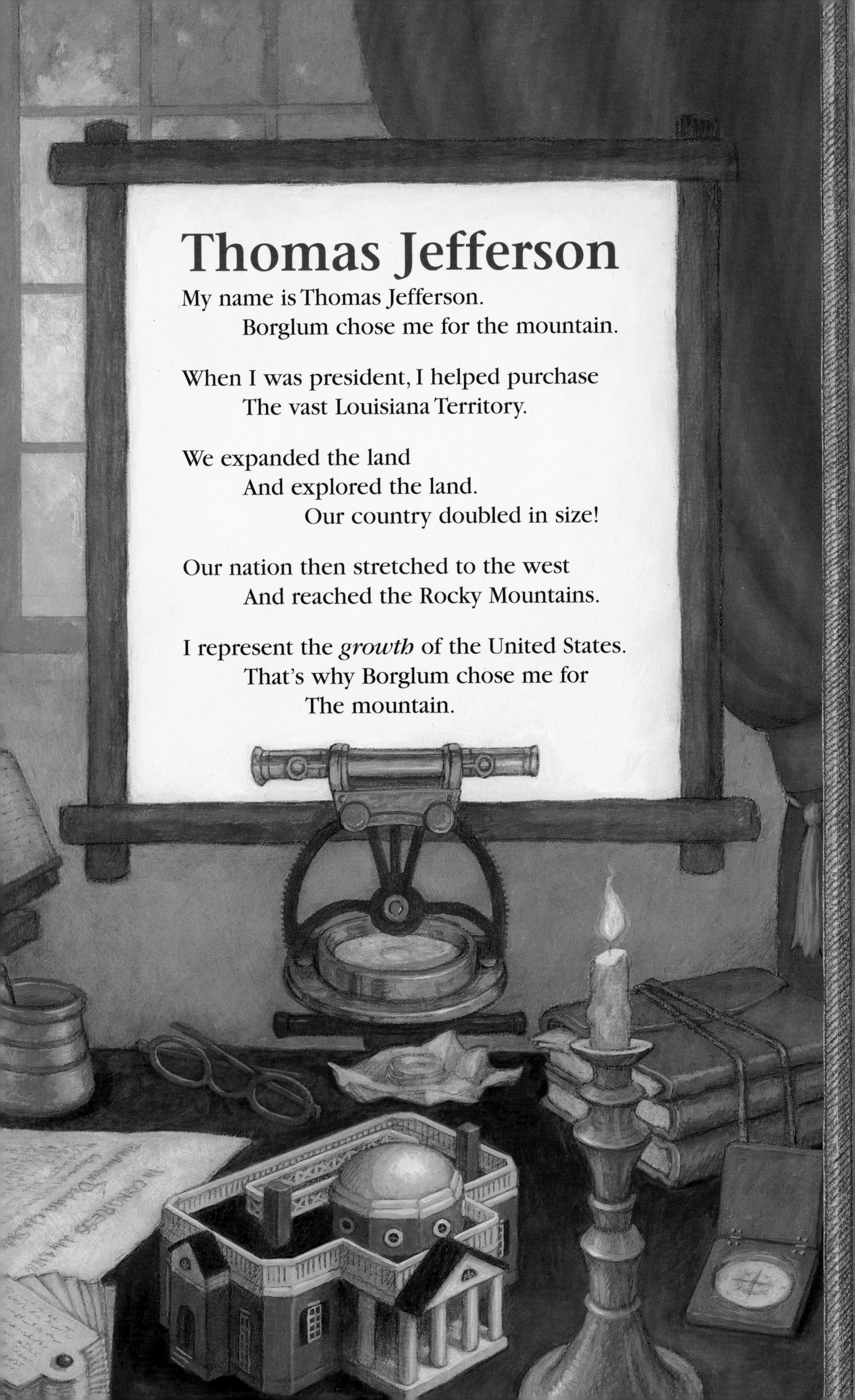

# Thomas Jefferson

My name is Thomas Jefferson.
    Borglum chose me for the mountain.

When I was president, I helped purchase
    The vast Louisiana Territory.

We expanded the land
    And explored the land.
        Our country doubled in size!

Our nation then stretched to the west
    And reached the Rocky Mountains.

I represent the *growth* of the United States.
    That's why Borglum chose me for
        The mountain.

## MORE OF THE STORY

BORN April 13, 1743
BIRTHPLACE Shadwell, Virginia
CHARACTERISTICS 6' 2½",
    freckles and reddish hair
DIED July 4, 1826
BURIED Monticello, near Charlottesville,
    Virginia

### Career Highlights

Wrote Declaration of Independence
in 1776.

Served as third president of the United
States from 1801 to 1809.

Purchased Louisiana Territory from France
for $15 million in 1803.

*"I cannot live without books."*
    – THOMAS JEFFERSON
    June 10, 1815

### Interesting Fact

Thomas Jefferson was an inventor.

He designed a swivel chair,
an adjustable music
stand, a plow,
and a portable
writing desk.

**Lewis & Clark Expedition:** Thomas
Jefferson authorized the Corps of Discovery
to further the scientific exploration of the
western United States.

# MORE OF THE STORY

BORN February 12, 1809

BIRTHPLACE One-room log cabin
near Hodgenville, Kentucky

CHARACTERISTICS 6' 4", long arms
and legs

DIED April 15, 1865
(assassinated)

BURIED Oak Ridge
Cemetery,
Springfield, Illinois

## Career Highlights

Served as sixteenth president of the United
States from 1861 to 1865.

Issued the Emancipation Proclamation
on January 1, 1863.

Declared freedom for slaves in territory
at war with the Union.

Presented Gettysburg Address on
November 19, 1863.

Explained that the Union must
continue the war to preserve democracy
and freedom.

Lincoln sometimes told jokes to take his
mind off the war. *"Were it not for this occa-
sional vent, I would die. I must laugh to keep
from crying."*

– ABRAHAM LINCOLN, 1861

## Interesting Story

Lincoln's son Tad once tied two goats to
a kitchen chair and drove them through
the White House.

**13th Amendment:** Abraham Lincoln signed
the 13th Amendment to the Constitution in
1865, which eventually freed the slaves.

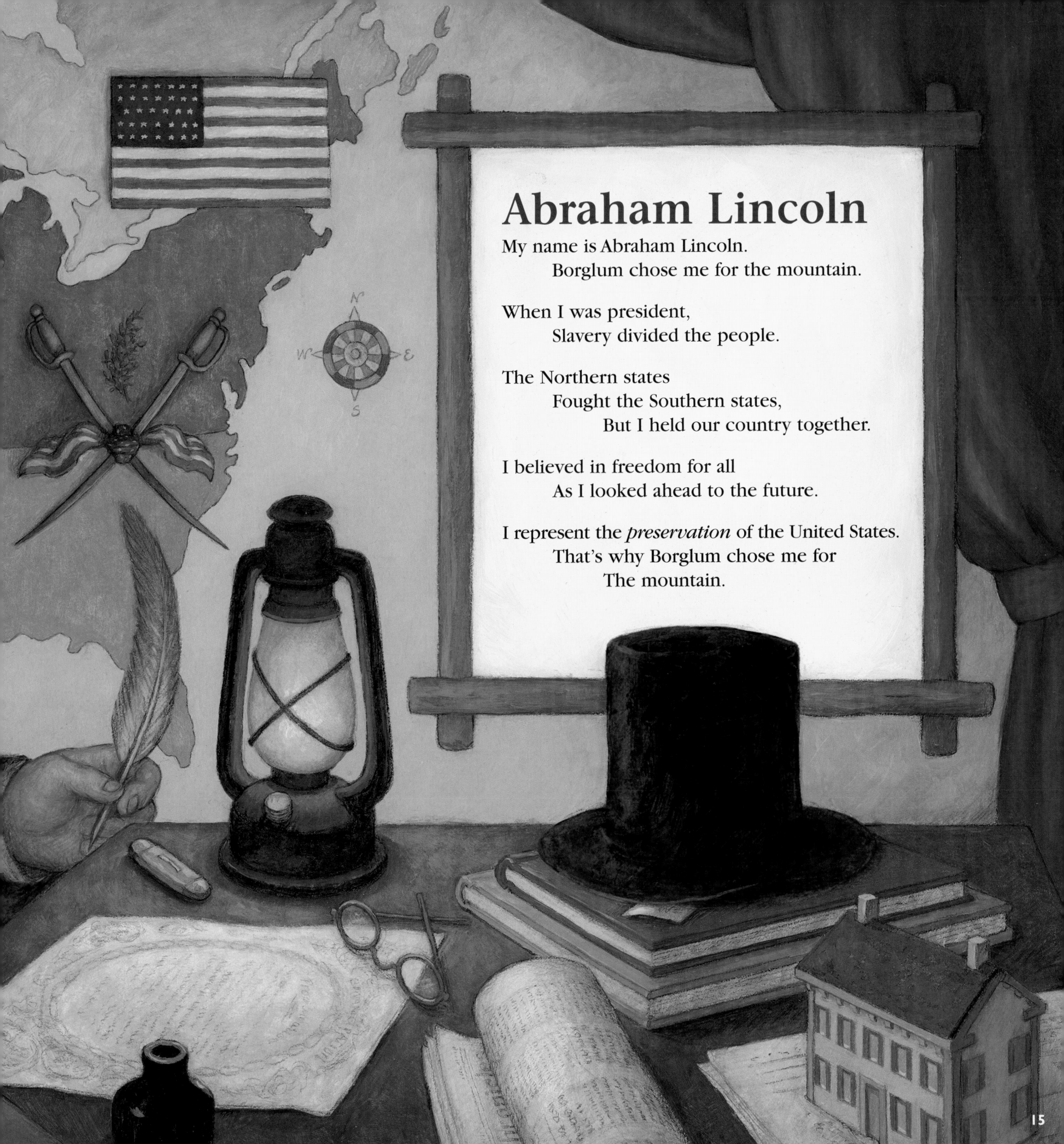

# Abraham Lincoln

My name is Abraham Lincoln.
>Borglum chose me for the mountain.

When I was president,
>Slavery divided the people.

The Northern states
>Fought the Southern states,
>>But I held our country together.

I believed in freedom for all
>As I looked ahead to the future.

I represent the *preservation* of the United States.
>That's why Borglum chose me for
>>The mountain.

# Theodore Roosevelt

My name is Theodore Roosevelt.
> Borglum chose me for the mountain.

When I was president,
> I began the Panama Canal.

The Atlantic Ocean
> Met the Pacific Ocean
>> With a fifty-mile pathway of water.

Our ships would use this shortcut
> To travel across the world.

I represent the *development* of the United States.
> That's why Borglum chose me for
>> The mountain.

Who helped Borglum carve these faces?

## MORE OF THE STORY

**BORN** October 27, 1858
**BIRTHPLACE** New York, New York
**CHARACTERISTICS** 5'8", wide grin
and moustache
**DIED** January 6, 1919
**BURIED** Oyster Bay, New York

### Career Highlights

Served as twenty-sixth president of the United States from 1901 to 1909.

Began construction of the Panama Canal in 1904, which provided a new route for trade ships and for the U.S. Navy.

Nicknamed the "Great Conservationist" as he established 150 National Forests, 5 National Parks, and 18 National Monuments.

*"It is true of the Nation, as of the individual, that the greatest doer must also be a great dreamer."*

– THEODORE ROOSEVELT, 1911

### Interesting Fact

Roosevelt's wife and mother died on February 14, 1884. Brokenhearted, he moved to Dakota Territory (current-day western North Dakota) where he ranched, hunted, and even captured an outlaw.

**Rough Riders:** Theodore Roosevelt led the Rough Riders in the Spanish American War in 1898.

## MORE OF THE STORY

Mount Rushmore was carved from 1927 to 1941.

**Measurements on the mountain**
EYES 11 feet across
NOSES 20 feet long
MOUTHS 18 feet across
FACES FROM FOREHEAD TO CHIN 60 feet
ENTIRE BODIES
   If carved full-length, each president would be 465 feet tall.

**The Pointing System**
The pointer made thousands of measurements. First, he measured the model with a long metal shaft and a plumb bob. Next, he multiplied each distance by twelve. Using red paint held in a tin cup, he transferred these distances to the mountain.

**More Changes**
While creating Mount Rushmore, Borglum made nine major changes to his models. With each change, the pointer had to measure the new model and put the new measurements on the mountain.

**Lincoln Borglum**
Gutzon Borglum's son Lincoln worked as a pointer.

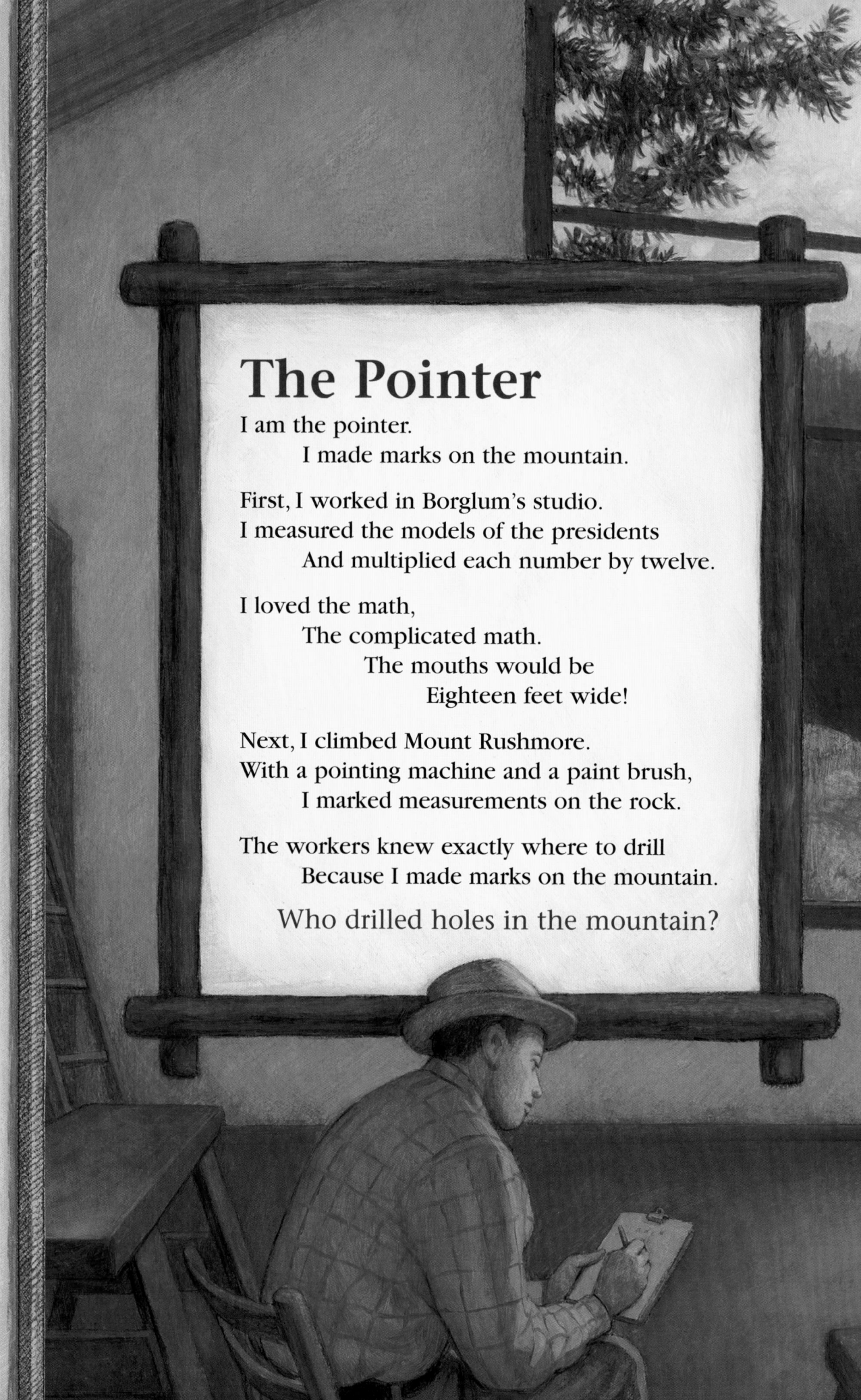

# The Pointer

I am the pointer.
　　　　I made marks on the mountain.

First, I worked in Borglum's studio.
I measured the models of the presidents
　　　　And multiplied each number by twelve.

I loved the math,
　　　　The complicated math.
　　　　　　　The mouths would be
　　　　　　　　　Eighteen feet wide!

Next, I climbed Mount Rushmore.
With a pointing machine and a paint brush,
　　　　I marked measurements on the rock.

The workers knew exactly where to drill
　　　　Because I made marks on the mountain.

Who drilled holes in the mountain?

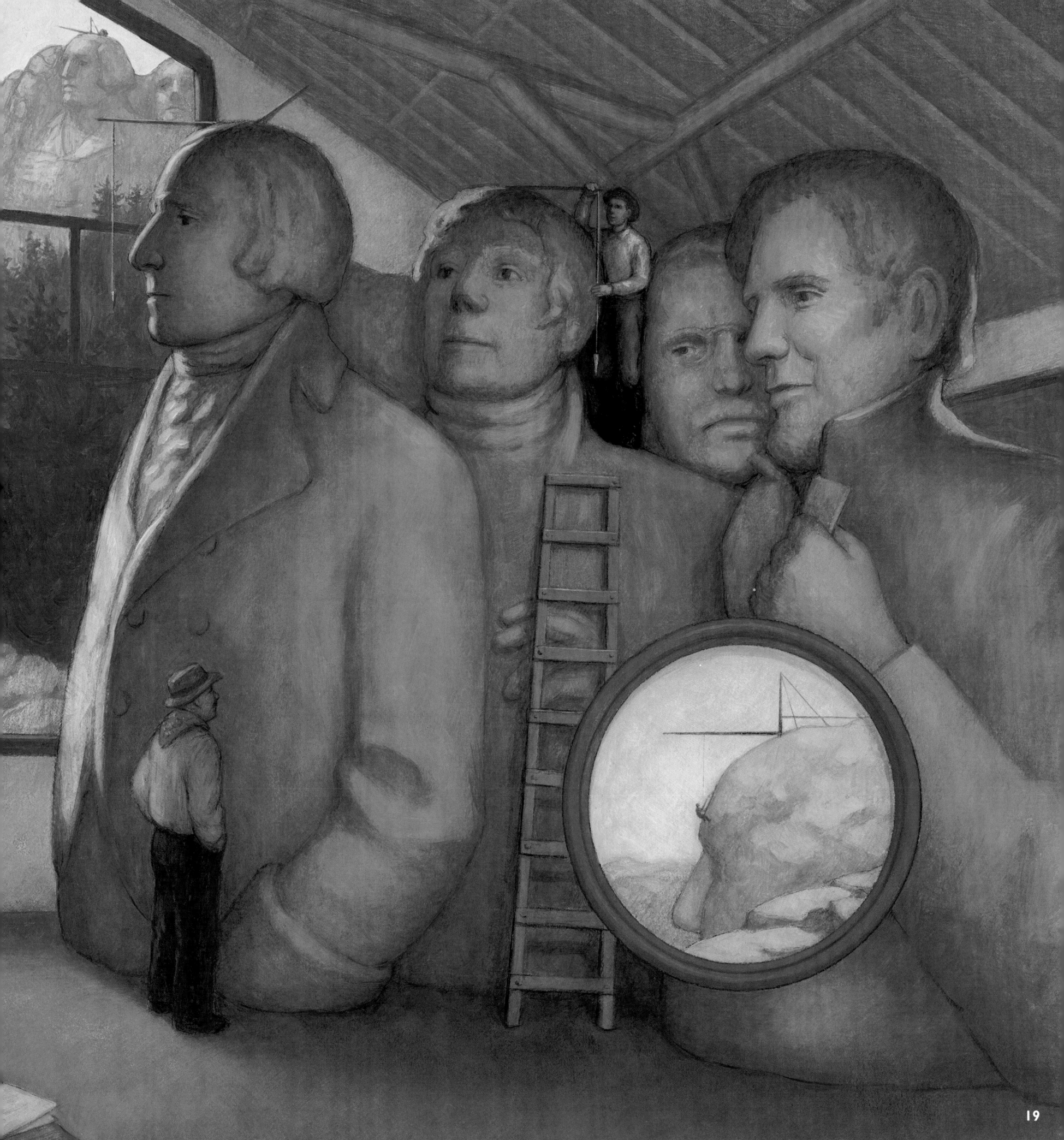

Winch
Man

Call boy

Steel
Nippers

Blacksmith
Shop

Cooks

# The Driller

I am the driller.
    I drilled long holes in the mountain.

Each morning, I'd tighten my harness,
    Take a deep breath, and walk backwards
        Off the mountain.

I hung from a cable,
    A thin steel cable.
        I leaned against the sky.

The sun was hot. The dust was sharp.
My jackhammer weighed eighty-five pounds!

I created a place for the dynamite
    As I drilled long holes in the mountain.

    Who was in charge of the dynamite?

## MORE OF THE STORY

### Workers on the Mountain

Approximately 400 men and women worked together to create Mount Rushmore.

The **winch man** lowered the driller at the end of a steel cable only ⅜" in diameter.

The **call boy** yelled to the winch man to lower or raise the driller.

The **steel nippers** moved up and down the mountain, delivering sharpened drill bits from the blacksmith who sharpened 400–500 drill bits each day.

**Women** cooked and cleaned in the dining hall, kitchen, and bunkhouse. Other workers built roads, did landscaping, and sold souvenirs. (The souvenirs were sold in Borglum's studio!)

### Strong Legs

Each morning, workers climbed over 700 stairs up the back of the cliff to get to the top of Mount Rushmore.

### Worker Wages

Payroll June 1, 1935
BLACKSMITH 75¢ per hour
CALL BOY 55¢ per hour
CHIEF CARVER $1.50 per hour
SENIOR DRILLER 75¢ per hour
CHIEF POINTER $1.00 per hour

### Bosun Chairs

Gutzon Borglum invented swing seats called "bosun chairs." When the workers were strapped into the steel and leather harnesses, it was impossible to fall out of them.

### Air Power!

Large compressors at the base of the mountain pushed air up a pipe and through hoses to give power to the pneumatic drills (often called jackhammers). The pipe was a half-mile long!

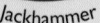
*Jackhammer*

**Nicknames**

Powder men were sometimes called "powder monkeys."

**Dynamite**

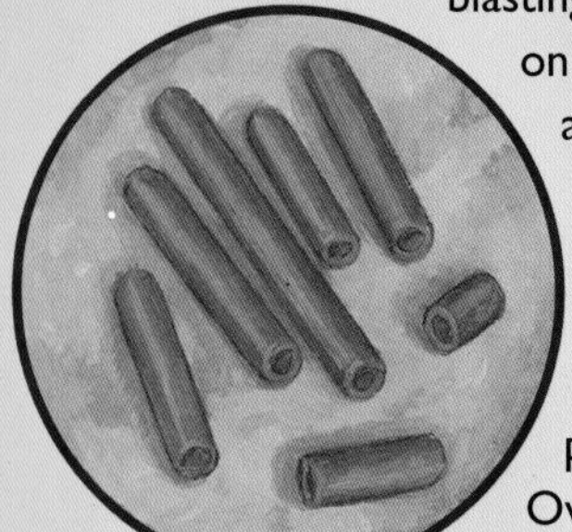

Many of Rushmore's workers had worked in the mines. They were used to drilling and blasting. The powder men on Rushmore were so accurate that they could blast off the rock to within inches of the final surface of the presidents' faces. Over 450,000 tons of granite were blasted off the mountain. You can still see the rubble on the talus slope below the mountain.

**Safety first**

No one ever died while working on the mountain. The blasts were fired during the lunch hour and at the end of the day when the workers were not on the cliff.

**Biggest Blast**

In 1934, Thomas Jefferson was carved to Washington's right. When Borglum realized the rock was weak, he ordered the workers to blast it off the mountain. Later, Jefferson was carved on the other side of Washington.

Detonator

# The Powder Man

I am the powder man.
    I blasted rock off the mountain.

At first, my work was quiet.
I cut the sticks of dynamite and
    Loaded them into the holes. Then …

Noontime: BOOOMMM!
    4:00: BOOOMMM!
        CRASH! SMASH! THUD!

Twice each day, I fired the blasts.
I shaped the heads with explosions.

But I needed help with the details
    After I blasted rock off the mountain.

Who carved the details on the faces?

### Detail Work

The process of drilling the rows of holes was called "honeycombing." The holes looked like the honeycomb of a beehive.

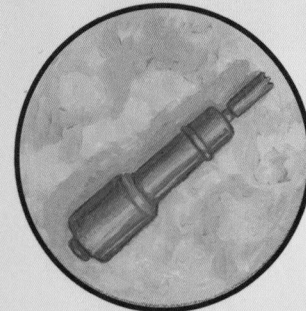

The small jackhammer was often called a "bumper."

### A Twinkle in the Eye

Gutzon Borglum told the carvers to leave a 20-inch shaft of granite in the center of each eye. The ends of these shafts would catch the sunlight and bring the presidents' eyes to life.

### The Final Stages

Borglum examined the faces from his studio, the valley, and even from the tram. Often he worked on the mountain, marking places where the faces should be shaped. Sometimes, he picked up the tools and showed workers the techniques he wanted. Borglum's subtle details gave the faces their personality.

# The Stone Carver

I am the stone carver.
    I carved details on the mountain.

I drilled rows and rows of shallow holes,
Then broke off the rock with a chisel.
With a small jackhammer and a four-star bit,
    I smoothed the rough surface of the faces.

Their stone expressions
    Became human expressions
        As I followed Borglum's commands.

I was sculpting the faces
    That would shine through the years
        To honor democracy and freedom.

But Borglum grew older,
    And his son took over
        As I carved details on the mountain.

Who was Borglum's son?

# Lincoln Borglum

I am Lincoln Borglum.
I am the boy who became the man
    Who completed the work on the mountain.

On March 6, 1941, my father —
    Gutzon Borglum — died.
I looked at the unfinished mountain.

I thought of his dream,
    His far-reaching dream,
        To show America to the future.

So I led the faithful workers.
We smoothed the skin on Roosevelt's face
    And the waves on Jefferson's hair.
We sculpted the side of Lincoln's head
    And finished Washington's collar.

I kept my father's dream alive
    As I completed the work on the mountain.

        Who shares this dream?

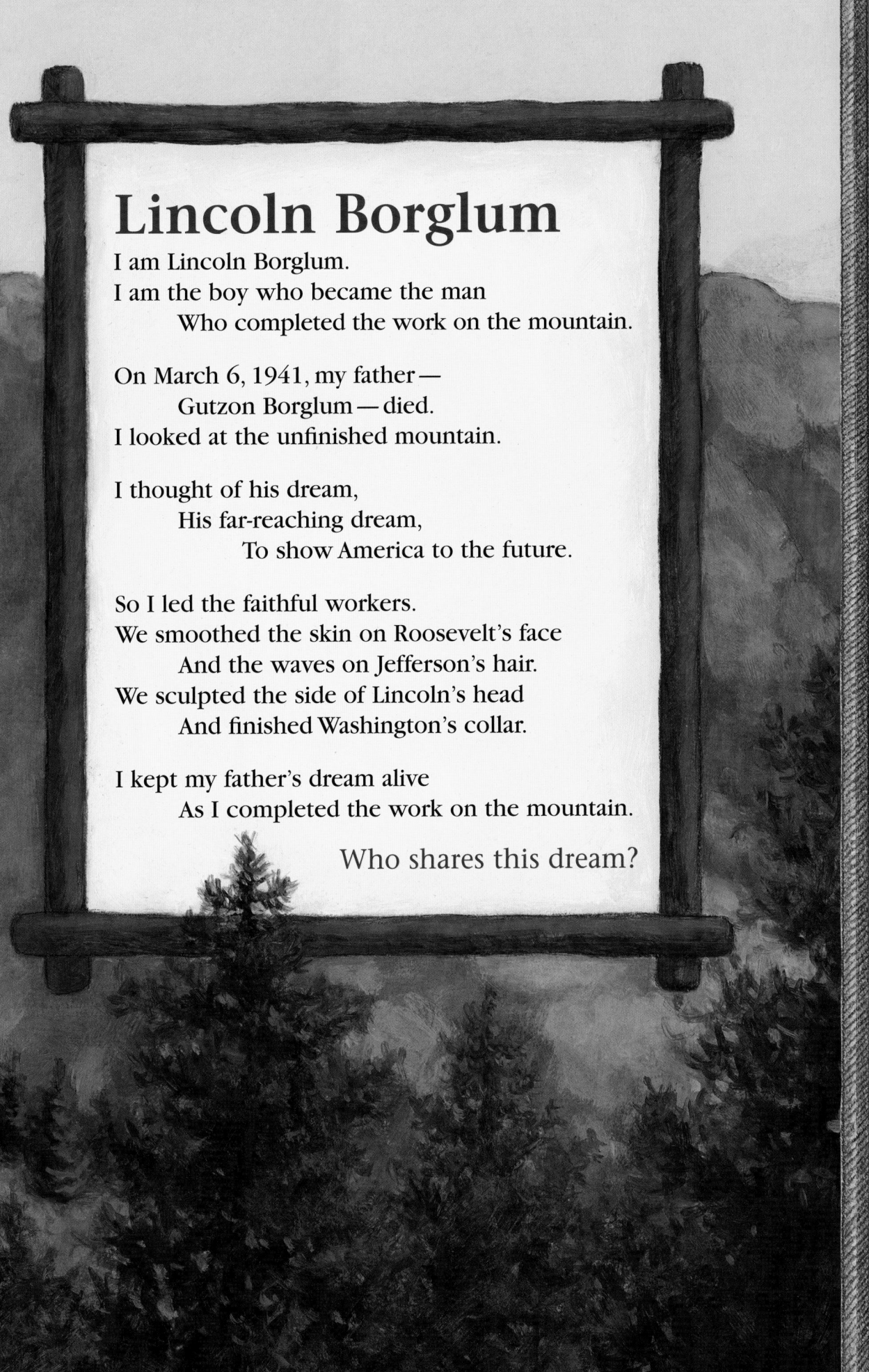

## MORE OF THE STORY

### World War II
Just five weeks after the carving was finished, Pearl Harbor was bombed. United States soldiers would fight to protect democracy.

### Unfinished Goals
Gutzon Borglum wanted people of the future to know about America. At first, he wanted to carve a 500-word history of the United States next to the faces. When the faces were carved, there was no room for this "Entablature."

He also had hoped to build a "Hall of Records" in the canyon behind the faces. He wanted the Hall to hold United States documents and explain the meaning of Mount Rushmore to future civilizations. A 75-foot-long tunnel was drilled, but Lincoln did not have money to complete it.

### Hall of Records Today
In 1998, Gutzon Borglum's daughter — Mary Ellis Borglum Vhay — helped accomplish the goal.

With the help of the National Park Service and the Mount Rushmore National Memorial Society, a special box was buried at the entrance to the cave. The box holds information about Mount Rushmore and the presidents. It also contains the words of the Declaration of Independence and the Constitution.

# We the People

We are the people.
        We share the dream of the mountain.

We come from all places to visit the faces
        That look across the land.

We think about our history.
        We think about our democracy.
                We are thankful for our freedom.

Our faces join
        Their faces
                As we look to the future.

We are the people of the mountain.

# The Story of the Presidents' Desks

The presidents' desks and offices, as illustrated in this book, show numerous objects that represent the times in which the presidents lived, as well as their hobbies, interests, and skills.

## Washington

1. American flag when Washington became president.
2. A map of the 13 colonies.
3. The Washington family coat of arms.
4. Washington enjoyed looking at the stars through a telescope.
5. A model of Mount Vernon, Washington's home in Virginia.
6. Washington's seal.
7. Washington loved to read.
8. Washington used his gavel as president of the Constitutional Congress.
9. The Constitution of the United States.
10. Washington's main light source.

## Jefferson

1. American flag when Jefferson became president.
2. A map showing how the Louisiana Purchase expanded the United States.
3. Jefferson invented a revolving bookstand to read five books at once.
4. Jefferson's peace medal that Lewis & Clark took on their expedition.
5. Jefferson invented the candlelit chair.
6. An orrery, mechanical representation of the solar system.
7. Jefferson took notes on ivory notebooks.
8. The Declaration of Independence.
9. A model of Monticello, Jefferson's home in Virginia.
10. A telescope theodolite used for surveying land.
11. Small books compact for traveling.
12. Jefferson's spectacles with a variety of lenses, including tinted.

## Lincoln

1. American flag when Lincoln became president.

2. A map showing the Mason-Dixon line between the North and South.

3. "Old Abe" was a live eagle that served as a mascot for the Northern troops during the Civil War.

4. Lincoln's main light source.

5. Lincoln was known for sticking notes in his hat.

6. A model of the home Lincoln lived in while in Illinois.

7. Lincoln liked to read newspapers.

8. Emancipation Proclamation.

## Roosevelt

1. American flag when Roosevelt became president.

2. Roosevelt loved the outdoors.

3. Roosevelt's life was saved when the glasses case in his pocket stopped an assassin's bullet in 1912.

4. A model of Sagamore, Roosevelt's home in New York.

5. Roosevelt had electric lights.

6. Roosevelt used the telephone.

7. A globe showing the trade routes made possible by the Panama Canal.

8. Roosevelt's Nobel Peace Prize of 1906.

9. The Sherman Antitrust Act.

# Timeline

**August 20, 1924**
Doane Robinson writes to Gutzon Borglum about carving a "massive sculpture" in the Black Hills.

**August 1925**
Borglum visits Black Hills again with his son, Lincoln. Theodore Shoemaker shows Mount Rushmore to Borglum. Borglum, Lincoln, and six others climb Mount Rushmore.

**December 1923**
67-year-old Doane Robinson has idea for carving the Needles.

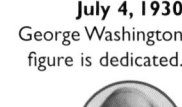

**July 4, 1930**
George Washington figure is dedicated.

**August 30, 1936**
Thomas Jefferson figure is dedicated.

**July 2, 1939**
Theodore Roosevelt figure is dedicated.

| 1920 | 1921 | 1922 | 1923 | 1924 | 1925 | 1926 | 1927 | 1928 | 1929 | 1930 | 1931 | 1932 | 1933 | 1934 | 1935 | 1936 | 1937 | 1938 | 1939 | 1940 | 1941 |

**September 1924**
57-year-old Gutzon Borglum visits Black Hills with 12-year-old son, Lincoln.

**August 10, 1927**
President Calvin Coolidge dedicates Mount Rushmore.

**October 4, 1927**
Actual drilling on Mount Rushmore begins.

**September 17, 1937**
Abraham Lincoln figure is dedicated.

**March 6, 1941**
Gutzon Borglum dies in Chicago hospital after minor surgery.

**October 31, 1941**
Carving on Mount Rushmore stops.

## The Money Story

**How much?** Mount Rushmore cost $989,992.32 ($153,992.32 from South Dakota business and other private sources; $836,000 from the U.S. government).

**Why?** Equipment and power needed to be purchased. Workers had to be paid. Work on Mount Rushmore often stopped because of lack of money.

**Who helped raise money?** South Dakota children raised $1,707.80 to help build Mount Rushmore. Grade school students gave their dimes. High school students contributed quarters.

South Dakota Senator **Peter Norbeck** and Representative **William Williamson** were among those who persuaded Congress to give hundreds of thousands of dollars to help pay for Mount Rushmore. Gutzon Borglum also helped raise money.

**John Boland** was in charge of the money for Mount Rushmore. He also was a businessman who sold farm implements in Rapid City, South Dakota.

## Selected Bibliography

Borglum, Gutzon. Letters to Major Harold P. Munck. September 19, 1927; September 27, 1927. Mount Rushmore National Memorial Archives.

Borglum, Lincoln. *My Father's Mountain*. Fenwinn Press, 1997.

Fite, Gilbert C. *Mount Rushmore*. Mount Rushmore History Association, 2003.

Griffith, T.D. *America's Shrine of Democracy: A Pictorial History*. Mount Rushmore National Memorial Society, 2004.

Higbee, Paul. *Mount Rushmore's Hall of Records*. Mount Rushmore History Association, 1999.

Lincoln Borglum Museum. Exhibits. Mount Rushmore National Memorial. January 2004.

Ostendorf, Lloyd. *Abraham Lincoln: The Boy, The Man*. Wagner, 1988.

Smith, Rex Alan. *The Carving of Mount Rushmore*. Abbeville Press, 1985.

Tucker, J.G. Daily Record of Progress Made on the National Memorial at Rushmore. September – December 1927. Mount Rushmore National Memorial Archives.

Worker Interviews. Glen Bradford, John Naugle, Emmet Oslund, Jack Payne. Mount Rushmore National Memorial Archives.

Yoder, Carolyn. *George Washington, The Writer: A Treasury of Letters, Diaries, and Public Documents*. Boyds Mills Press, 2003.